DEAR ZUZI<u>K</u>

WE HOPE T

MAKE YOU FEEL GOOD

& RELAX WHILE

REEDING ALL

THE WAY TO

THE END.

IT'S SOMETHING VERY

DIFFERENT SO HAVE

A GO & ENJOY IT!

ⵣ

<u>LoVe</u>

The Inkspot Monologues

The Inkspot Monologues

KEITH POINTING

WORD OF MOUTH

As the leading dysfunctional relationship therapist, I use the Rorschach Inkblot Test to encourage patients to exorcise their romantic pasts. Alice and Jack tell their stories.

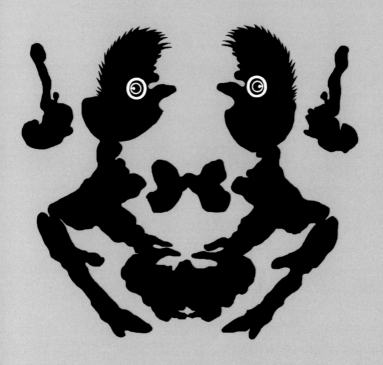

Alice

This bit on the left is, I think, Jonathan. I like the strong silent type. Jonathan was so strong on silence, it was difficult to get a word out of him.

Jonathan's idea of 'Going out' didn't actually involve leaving the house, just going from one room to another. We had what I thought was the beginning of 'a relationship', but it wasn't exactly 'physical'. I decided to bring up the subject, saying I thought we should try becoming 'closer'.

'We should try "making love!"' he said, 'but only if doesn't involve touching'.

Jonathan could have been called introverted.

However, Jonathan was not too introverted to go off with that Philippa Stevens. What he saw in that Philippa Stevens, I've no idea. Yes, she looked cute, but everyone will tell you...

Philippa was just about the biggest bitch

you've ever seen in your entire life.

I've never had trouble attracting boys. Getting rid of them is usually the problem. Dominic was one such specimen. He sidled up to me one day in a bar and stuck to me like a limpet. I try to be as open-minded as anyone when it comes to personal idiosyncrasies and little peccadilloes. When he knew me slightly more, he said he wanted to tell me something and would I try to understand. So, he says...

'I have a knickers collection as big as yours'. Guess what:
it was mine. Dominic *was* really creepy.

Jack

I see a woman's leg and another and there, another. I adore women. And you know, I am *not* difficult. Just unlucky. Take Vicky: Vicky had wonderful legs that were so long they gave me vertigo. But that was almost all there was to her. Very little up top, and a man can't live by legs alone.

Vicky had fantastic legs,

but the rest you could keep.

Then there was Samantha. Samantha was naturally proud of her amazing breasts.

Samantha had great breasts, but everything else about her was revolting.

Alice

Norman meant well, but then he kept saying things like, 'I'm a happening kind a guy' or 'I'm one of the most romantic people that you could ever meet and I want to show you the world's great wide open spaces'. Sadly, I soon realized the only space I would ever see was the one between his ears.

Norman was simply a drip.

And Craig? His self-importance was eventually his undoing.

Shane's advice was, 'always put your best foot forward', which was bit rich coming from him: He hadn't a clue where to look for his best foot.

Shane was really mixed up.

Vince had this all-consuming relationship with his mother. She couldn't let go. 'My little boy's 1,937 weeks old now', she would say.

Deryk wanted to be my 'man about the house', but his D.I.Y. obsession included his attitude to sex...

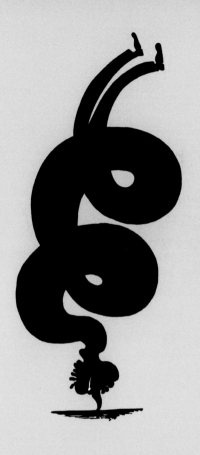

While he was great at plumbing, plastering and fixing,

Deryk himself needed rewiring. Deryk screwed up.

Jack

I was hoping to meet a girl who'd drive me wild with uncontrollable passion and crazy with unbelievable lust – I wanted a woman who would corrupt and deprave me. Instead, I met Sandra. Sandra, with her sensible shoes, her sensible hairstyle, and her sensible clothes. And Sex – well that was out of the question; it wouldn't have been sensible. How did I cope? By drinking myself insensible.

After I dried out, I met Daisy, but...

Daisy was so neurotic, that she got on everyone's
nerves, including her own.

Daisy was irritating, but Virginia was all, 'Do you like my dress?' (BUZZ) 'Really... go on.' (BUZZ) 'Do you like it?' (BUZZ) 'Does it go with my shoes?' (BUZZ) 'Or does it make me look fat?' (BUZZ) 'What's the matter with you?' (BUZZ) 'Why don't you pay attention to me any-more?' (BUZZ) 'Come on. Let's talk...' (BUZZZZ)

Virginia was really, really, *really* annoying.

Alice

Size is always an issue, and certainly some girls say size matters. In Hugo's case finding anything at all was the problem. From every aspect...

...Hugo was totally insignificant.

While Gerald, once a 'bright young thing',

became one enormous 'thing'.

Then I seemed to attract guys for whom Anger Management courses were created. In the beginning Toby was charming, easy-going and debonair. Then he completely changed. Everyone's stress levels went off the Richter scale the moment he walked into a room. 'Why ask when you can argue?' he would say, or 'Why converse when you can confront?' He saw a simple 'Good morning' as an act of provocation. To put it mildly...

Toby had embarrassing out-bursts.

Being able to laugh at life's difficulties is essential in any successful relationship. Kev said he had 'a good sense of humour'. Over the next few days, he flicked bogeys at my mother, mooned at my girlfriends, and gave a dance for my granny that involved balloons, no clothes and farting.

Kev thought he was a comedian.

Dan was a one-man weather front; when he came in to a room, a black cloud would descend over everyone else.

Dan had horrible moods.

Jack

Laura had the classic 'passive-aggressive' personality, which always made her prickly.

Some people have a fear of being naked amongst colleagues, while others fear soiling the carpet. Gillian's neurosis was completely different...

Gillian didn't so much suffer from Penis Envy,

as began to look like one...

... which wasn't helped by that perm.

Samantha! Who cares that romantic love is an illusion, a chemical trick played by genes to ensure reproduction? Not me, when Samantha came along. Samantha was a peach!

But then she changed, and everything about our relationship, including her, went pear-shaped.

And last I heard, Samantha had gone all 'fruity'.

All the boys buzzed around Bridget like bees round a honey pot. The trouble was Bridget didn't believe in sex before marriage... nor afterwards.

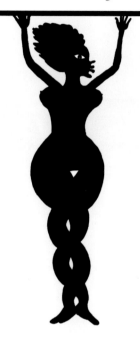

No. Thank you.

Bridget was frigid.

Alice

I've been out with some right psychos, weirdoes, oddballs and sleazebags. Raymond was one of the worst. He claimed to be the sexiest man alive. Well, he was certainly really dirty; I found mice droppings in his pubes. And he had the cheek to tell me that I was 'the apple of his eye', but...

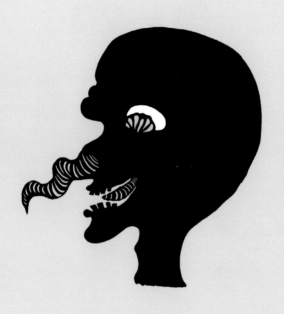

Raymond was rotten to the core.

Den was undoubtedly very charming, but you had to be really careful if he invited you for a drink after work, and you could never go round his place for dinner in the evening...

Den would have eaten you for breakfast.

I spent the next few weeks trying to avoid guys like Den and Peter. Peter, with his champagne for breakfast, even when I hadn't asked for any, truffles for lunch, chocolates for tea, and oily hand up my arse...

Peter was too smooth by half.

Philip said he had the 'biggest apartment, the biggest car, the biggest salary and the biggest penis'...

Philip was big headed.

Jack

When we first met, Gwendoline was very sweet: She was a 'poor little damsel in distress' and I was her 'knight in shining armour'.

But she had such a temper, she could even give

Saint George a run for his money.

My life was quieter, but also a little empty, until Louise, who claimed to be 'serious', 'intellectual', and 'spiritual'. At last, I'd found my soul-mate; someone with whom I could have a deep and proper relationship. But she meant 'serious' as in 'serious about shopping', 'intellectual' as in 'I shop, therefore I am' and 'spiritual' as in...

'Shopping really does fulfil my very deepest

spiritual needs.'

Alice

Leon was certainly plausible. He was all alone and there was no one else in his world but me, he said. Which was strictly true, if you discount his wife, five children, two dogs and budgie. He was very interested in 'personal finance' – by which he meant mine. And when we parted he said that he wanted to leave me something very special: that turned out to be just nasty letters from the bank...

Leon was a twister.

No matter what dress I tried on, Stephen would say that I looked 'wonderful'. He'd then always insist on buying it, even if I didn't like it. Stephen just worshiped the ground I walked on, which really got on my nerves.

Stephen was a complete crawler.

Now Stuart, he was a *real* man, but...

I never called Stuart narcissistic.

He wouldn't have known what it meant.

Bob's success went entirely to his head. At least, that was his excuse for the drinking.

Keiran was always talking about saving the whales, saving the forests, saving the planet, saving the universe, saving everything but time for me....

Keiran always had other things on his mind.

When I can remember going to several clubs, theatres and restaurants, accompanied, but I can't remember with whom, then I know it almost certainly would have been with John. John had such a lack of personality that I have trouble recalling almost anything he said, and the little I can was so predicable that I was always able to finish what he had started. He was a professional, in law, accounts, statistics or something like that. He did seem to have several friends, but I can't remember any of their names.

John was too ordinary.

I'm sure there is a nice girl somewhere out there for John. Nice – but a bit boring.

But at least with John, I can remember being awake for most of the time. Which is more than can be said for Daniel, who was so boring he not only cured me of my insomnia...

I actually developed narcolepsy.

I tried the personals. "'No time wasters', please', my ad said. So in one sense I was really lucky with Graham. He was the solid and dependable type. Well, certainly solid from the neck up, and unfortunately so dependable you could set your watch by him. He told me he had come to a decision and it was 'time that we went out. At one o'clock we shall have a three-course lunch for two. At one-twenty-three, we'll then have coffee and mints and at forty-five minutes past the hour we shall have a romantic walk, clockwise, around the lake during which time I'd like to discuss the importance of punctuality'. In his company, time wasn't exactly wasted but seemed to last an eternity.

Graham had no imagination.

Max. You had to hand it to Max – you could always reply on him to put his foot in it.

Robert wasn't sure if he should be a circus performer or an accountant. He settled for an accountant who wished he was a circus performer. Or was it the other way around?

Robert had an identity crisis...

...which was nothing compared to Patrick, who claimed to be a 'bi-lesbo-trans-straight-homo-trannie-gay kind of guy'.

It would be unfair to label James a 'commitment phobe', because he wasn't sure about anything. He had to check the mirror to make sure he wasn't a figment of his own imagination.

James was consumed with self doubt.

Jack

Fay didn't put the cap back on the toothpaste. Left the bathroom soaking wet. Lipstick smeared all over the walls. Eyeliner trodden in the floor. Never made the bed. Didn't put her clothes away: left shoes, dirty knickers and used sanitary towels everywhere. Was always, always hours late, even after we'd had a huge flaming row and never ever swept, dusted, cleaned or ironed.

Fay was a big mess.

Alice

Julian was very keen. He said my knee-caps were the most erotic he'd ever seen, for a woman; wrote an ode to my tonsils and sent to my mother; said I reminded him of someone, but he couldn't remember who; and that he loved me as a sister, but one he had the 'hots' for.

Julian was completely out of his mind.

In some respects Roderick was well-grounded, except for one part of his anatomy...

Roderick had a wandering eye which the rest of his
body had the unfortunate habit of following.

Alex then came onto the scene. He was rich, had a great sense of humour and was attentive to my personal needs. Unfortunately, he also wanted to attend to just about every girl's personal needs...

Alex couldn't keep his hands to himself.

Nick was sensitive. Soap opera plots would reduce him to tears. He'd stay up all night worrying as to why he couldn't sleep with the light off. Nick turned stress into a way of life.

Vince admitted he was complicated...

but I was never going to straighten him out.

When I first knew Luke, he had everything. Then it all began to go: his looks, jobs, money, friends, hair, teeth.

Luke was a loser.

Zac was alright, but far too attached to his family.

Lawrence said 'I'm a very moral person and the trouble is that these days no one knows the difference between right and wrong, or good and bad.' But what he meant was 'right hair-cut, wrong shoes' or 'good shirt, bad tie' ...

Lawrence was a hopeless lightweight.

And Kenny went out of control.

Jack

With Natalie, the attraction was instant. My very being was gorged with desire. But although she satisfied my deepest sexual desires, the problem was that Natalie claimed she had an eating disorder...

yeah, like 'men' and in whatever shape, size or colour she could get her hands on.

After we broke up, Natalie was really upset, saying that she needed me – which I took to mean as in comfort food between her next snack.

Belinda was at first a svelte size six, but almost over-night, a little cellulite became a lot of cellu-heavy and she...

became so huge, that sharing a bed began to be positively dangerous and ended up a physical impossibility. Belinda didn't so much just let herself go as went...

...everywhere.

Rose was rather charming,

but she had a butterfly mind.

And fluttered off with a bloke called Tom.

Alice

All Tom's previous girlfriends weren't up to the job. They weren't intelligent, beautiful, monied or sexy enough. So it was something of a coup that I even caught his eye and that he *actually* asked me out was absolutely incredible... at least that's what he told me...

Tom invented the superiority complex.

I liked Gazza, but he was never at ease with himself.

Although Simon looked normal, his problems were never far behind him.

Simon couldn't shake off his past.

Jack

Melinda believed in fate. Our love was written in the stars. But Melinda developed an obsession with all things cosmological, which descended to, 'No we can't have sex: Venus and Uranus aren't aligned.'

Melinda was an astrological bore.

Sally had a father fixation, while...

Elizabeth, although very patriotic,

was unbelievably ugly.

And you couldn't take her anywhere.

Lucy loved travelling but had
far too much personal baggage.

Alice

I like a man who is in touch with the inner self and isn't afraid to express his real feelings, who is honest and sees life for all it's creative possibilities and isn't afraid to experiment. Stanley was a little too honest, creative and experimental. Stanley, thought even the most inanimate objects had a certain sexual frisson. 'I just love the vibrations that come from your fridge.' He'd say, 'look at the legs on that table!' and 'Alice, I'm trying to be honest here. It's your cat – she's *very* tactile and is always looking at me in that *special way*. I think she might want more from me than is conventional in a traditional homo-feline relationship. I'm a generous person. I want to give. How would you feel about a threesome?'

Stanley had unusual tastes.

Everyone said it was so obvious. Anyone could see the moment they set eyes on him. I must have been completely crazy; an absolute fool. I realise it all now, oh so very clearly...

Percival was a mistake.

And Leslie was confused by his sexual identity...

...from the very beginning.

Mike was never there.

Jack

Matilda loved casting her spells and generally terrifying the menfolk; just one of her looks could shrivel my libido at 500 paces.

Linda became ever smaller, ever wider and bouncy.

Jade was cruel and vicious with a really nasty sting but no match for...

Sasha, who thought she was a knockout.

Alice

'I'm your spiritual guide.' Oz said. 'I will help you reach new heights and take you to another level of enlightenment and sexual fulfilment, after which your life will never be the same again.'

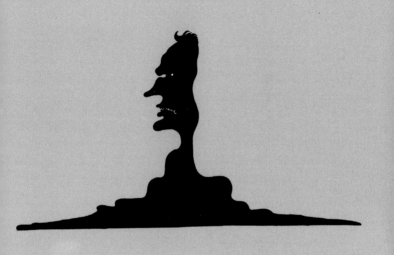

But Oz collapsed.

Dylan loved living at home. 'Why should I leave home', he said, 'when daddy gives me pocket money and mummy irons all my shirts?' If he did leave, where would he put his toy collection? All day he would play with his computer games, read his comics, and those 'lad's mags'...

Dylan couldn't grow up.

Bored with toy-boys in general, I thought I'd try the older, wiser man, which is how I met Gilbert. 'A 52 year age gap is nothing these days, is it?' Gilbert said. 'And what's more my piles are clearing up, my dandruff's much better and I've a new set of teeth.' Gilbert described himself as 'mature': 'Gone off' was a better description. 'I'm with it', he said. With 'what' he didn't explain...

Gilbert was past it.

Jack

I'm not afraid of commitment. But Jane said to me that, 'We will have a spring wedding in a pretty country church, with a full choir. The bridesmaids will have flowers entwined in their hair and be dressed in the best silk. The wedding breakfast will be a full eight courses, accompanied by string quartet, and of course, we'll have proper napkins. We'll leave for our honeymoon in a white Rolls-Royce. By the way, what did you say your name was?'

From the beginning, Jane was too clingy.

Alice

Mohammed and I had some great times together. He was such a laugh. But sometimes we change. We all do. Mohammed changed. And I could accept, in fact, I encouraged Mohammed, when he re-discovered his roots – his faith, which he took very seriously, even when he had, in his own words, become a Fundamentalist. This I could accept. And eventually, although it was at odds with much of what he had said he believed in, and many friends found it very strange, upsetting and definitely weird, I stood by him and also accepted his interest in... cross-dressing. But what really finished it for me, for the hurt and pain it caused, not only to himself, but to the others who had to look at him, for the wasted hours, the days he devoted to that, that...

body-building.

Geoffrey was ridiculous, but friendly.

Jack

Beth was interesting to talk to, well-read and amusing, but Beth and food were not a pretty sight.

Beth was a grotesque eating machine.

Desperation was beginning to set in when I met Susan. Initially Susan was charming, quiet, demure, considerate, and interested in me. But so incessant, powerful and ferocious became her nagging that if it in some way could be harnessed, it would be one of the most powerful natural forces known to man. In the end...

Susan couldn't whisper.

Alice

By the time I took up with Brian I was becoming desperate. Brian, however, made me feel very comfortable. He really boosted my ego, because Brian was a looker. They say you should never judge a book by its cover, but in Brian's case he was gorgeous! Everyone agreed, he had lips like rose-petals bathed in sunrays, eyes like almonds lit by moon-beams, a mind like, er...ummm, err, um...

Brian was beautiful, but brainless.

Jake 'thought' about
fondling my breasts,

Jake 'considered' tickling my
tonsils with his tongue,

Jake 'agonised' about
nibbling my neck...

Jake 'philosophised'
too much.

In some ways Ashley and I had a perfect relationship. We never went out, preferring cozy nights in. He didn't have much to say and was a really good listener. But I never guessed he was dead.

Jack

And Gabriella was just too 'nice'.

Alice

And they say nice guys always finish last.

Josh wasn't even nice.

Alice and Jack

So we thought, 'why don't we two give it a go?'!

THE END

FOR ROSEMARY, WILLIAM AND OLIVIA

The Inkspot Monologues
First published in Great Britain in 2009 by Word of Mouth Press
An imprint of Can of Worms Enterprises Limited
7 Peacock Yard, Iliffe Street, London SE17 3LH

Tel: +44 (0)20 7708 2942
Email: info@canofwormsenterprises.co.uk

Websites:
http://www.canofwormsenterprises.co.uk
http://inkspotmonologues.com

ISBN: 978-0-956011-90-9

British Library Cataloguing in Publication Data
A catalogue record for this book is available from the British Library

Design by Keith Pointing